The Little Witch's Summertime Book

by Linda Glovach

PRENTICE-HALL, INC., Englewood Cliffs, New Jersey

To all of my summertime friends,
and my Mother,
Julius, and Boo.

Copyright © 1986   by Linda Glovach

Printed in Spain   ·J

Prentice-Hall International (UK) Limited, London
Prentice-Hall of Australia, Pty. Ltd., Sydney
Prentice-Hall Canada, Inc., Toronto
Prentice-Hall Hispanoamericana, S.A., Mexico
Prentice-Hall of India Private Ltd., New Delhi
Prentice-Hall of Japan, Inc., Tokyo
Prentice-Hall of Southeast Asia Pte. Ltd., Singapore
Whitehall Books Limited, Wellington, New Zealand
Editora Prentice-Hall do Brasil LTDA., Rio de Janeiro

10 9 8 7 6 5 4 3 2 1

Library of Congress Cataloging in Publication Data

Glovach, Linda.
   The little witch's summertime book.
   Summary: Presents instructions for a variety of
summer activities, games, foods, and handicrafts.
   1. Handicraft–Juvenile literature.   2. Gardening–
Juvenile literature.   3. Cookery–Juvenile literature.
4. Summer–Juvenile literature. [1. Handicraft.
2. Cookery. 3. Summer] I. Title.
TT160.G548 1986   790.1'922   85-25750
ISBN 0-13-538018-9

Contents

INTRODUCTION

Summer is a very special time in the Little Witch's neighborhood. School is over and the Little Witch and her friends are busy doing many things. They set up a Summer Puppet Theater (p. 8), with characters like Helga the Hen, Wilson the Wise Owl, and Waldo the Wolf. They decide to hold a Summertime Country Fair (p. 18) and make all-purpose Pet Pigs to sell as banks, cookie jars, and lunch boxes. The Goblin shares some mouth-watering recipes from his kitchen. There is a Lazy Summer Day Cloud Picnic (don't forget to wear your Upside-Down Cloud Hat and bring your favorite book).

   The Little Witch and her friends love parties, so they play a Night Owl Party and Firefly Ball with Firefly Snacks, and a Fourth of July Sparkle Party that ends with Grandmother Witch's Summer Night Sherbet.

   If you get a summer cold, the Little Witch has some homemade recipes, like Honeybee Cookies, and special get-well cards to cheer you up. The Little Witch and the Goblin show you how to make a Frog on a Lily Pad and a Turtle out of easy-to-find shells from your summer beachcombing. Last but not least, the Little Witch shares some of her TOMBSTONE THRILLERS to make things spooky during summer thunderstorms!

THE LITTLE WITCH'S SUMMERTIME SAFETY CODE

Here are a few Summertime Safety suggestions to remember if you are going to be busy with the crafts, recipes, and activities in this book.

1. Always ask permission before starting a craft or activity and before planning a party. And remember to clean up after your fun. Don't leave a mess for others.

2. If you are cooking, and a stove, grill, or knife is needed, always ask an adult to help.

3. Do not go into the woods to have your picnic unless you know the area or have permission. A park or school playground under a shady tree is better. Watch out for poison ivy or other weeds that might give you a rash if you touch them. If you suffer a bee sting or insect bite, show your parent or sitter so it can be treated.

4. When you are collecting shells, be sure they do not contain live creatures. Do not touch jellyfish, sea urchins, etc. They might sting you or you may hurt them. Do not go into the water without a lifeguard present and always swim with a friend.

5. Avoid sunburn by staying out of the hot sunshine during the middle of the day, especially near water. Drink lots of water or other liquids on hot days.

LITTLE WITCH'S
IMPORTANT SUMMER EVENTS

Puppet Theater
Country Fair

THE LITTLE WITCH'S SUMMER PUPPET THEATER

Early in the summer, the Little Witch and her friends get busy organizing their Summer Puppet Theater. They make their own puppets, rehearse the play, prepare the stage, and put on the show! If you would like to have a Summer Puppet Theater in your neighborhood, follow the Little Witch's directions. You can put on a play almost anywhere—the park, the schoolyard, a church, block party, summer camp, or wherever you can get space. The Little Witch has hers in her own backyard.

Get together with all your friends who would like to participate in the theater. If there are only two or three of you, each person can play more than one part.

Each person should make the puppet characters he or she wants to be. Here is the Summer Puppet Theater cast:

Helga the Hen
Wilson the Wise Owl
Waldo the Wolf

Alex the Alligator
The Good Witch
King Tree Troll and the
Terrible Tree Trolls

Most of your puppets can be made from craft felt. You can buy it in a variety store or craft shop for about 39¢ a sheet. You can also use heavyweight construction paper if you staple the edges firmly. You can always make another puppet if the first one tears. The same puppets can be used in many different plays that you and your friends make up.

NOW MAKE YOUR PUPPETS

For Helga the Hen, *you need:* a 9″ × 12″ piece of white or beige craft felt; three 1″ × 5″ strips, two 2¼″ × 3″ pieces, three 4″ × 3½″ pieces, and two 2½″ × 3″ pieces of orange construction paper; two 1¼″ × 1¾″

pieces of green or blue construction paper; two 3¾″ × 2¾″ pieces of yellow construction paper; paints, scissors, stapler, white glue.

Fold the 9″ × 12″ piece of felt in half. All puppets when folded should be 6″ × 9″. With scissors, round off top corners as in picture. Staple closed all along top and side (not bottom).

Draw an oval shape on each 1¼″ × 1¾″ green or blue piece and cut out to make eyes. Paint pupils black, as in picture. Glue to puppet about 2″ down from top. Draw one triangle on each 2¼″ × 3″ orange piece and cut out. Fold each flat end over to form a ¼″ flap. Glue only the two flaps together, one on top of the other as in the picture. Then glue flap to hen below eyes for beak. Press firmly in place. Let glue set 20 minutes before you move beak up and down.

Roll up the three 1″ × 5″ strips to form tight cylinders. Hold in place, then release to form curls. Staple end of each strip to top of head (see picture). To make wings: Draw the crescent moon shape with scallops across the bottom on each 3¼″ × 2¾″ yellow piece. Cut out and staple one to each side of body.

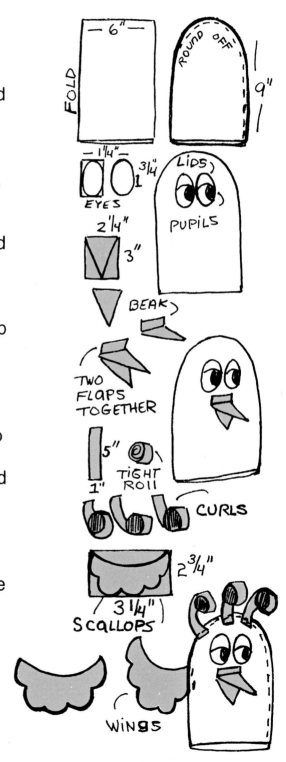

To make tail feathers: Draw the full crescent moon shape with scalloped bottom on each 4″ × 3½″ orange piece. Cut out. Place one piece on top of the other to make three overlapping layers, as in picture. Staple all together at one end. Make a flap at base of feathers and staple tail to back of hen about 2″ up from the bottom.

To make feet: On each 2½″ × 3″ orange piece, measure ¾″ in from the corners and mark dots. From dots, measure ½″ down, mark with dots again. From those dots, draw three small triangles, as in picture, with each point touching the edges of the paper. Cut out. Staple each triangle to front of puppet at bottom. (Staple the feet to front piece only, so you can slip your hand inside to move the puppet.)

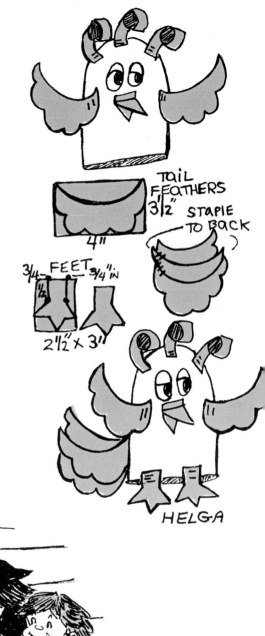

TAIL FEATHERS 3½″ STAPLE TO BACK

4″

FEET ¾″ IN

2½″ × 3″

HELGA

WILSON THE WISE OWL

You need: a 9″ × 12″ piece of brown craft felt; two 7½″ × 8″ pieces of orange construction paper; two 1¼″ × 1¾″ and two 1½″ × 2½″ pieces of yellow construction paper; two 2½″ × 3″ and two 1½″ × 1½″ pieces of brown construction paper; paint, scissors, stapler, white glue.

Make the basic 6″ × 9″ puppet body of Wilson by folding the 9″ × 12″ piece of felt in half, as you did for Helga the Hen. Draw triangles on the 1½ × 1½″ brown pieces and cut out. Staple triangles to top of body for ears. Draw oval eyes on the 1¼″ × 1¾″ yellow pieces and cut out. Paint black pupils. Glue to puppet for eyes. Make Owl's beak triangles exactly as you did for Helga the Hen, using the two 1½″ × 2½″ yellow pieces. Attach two halves of beak and glue to Owl the same way.

For wings: Mark a dot at top middle of each 7½″ × 8″ orange piece. Draw a line to bottom to divide each piece in half. From top dot out to ends on each half, make jagged zigzag lines like a Christmas tree, as in picture. Cut out on lines. Fold in half. Cut a curve along straight bottoms, so wings will fit better. Staple one wing to each side of Owl.

Make feet from the 2½″ × 3″ brown pieces, the same as for Helga the Hen (p. 10). Staple to front. Paint black "V" and "U" shaped feathers on front and back of Wilson.

11

WALDO THE WOLF

You need: one 9″ × 12″ piece and one 6″ × 3″ piece of gray or black craft felt; two 2″ × 2½″ pieces of gray or black construction paper; two 1″ × ½″ pieces of white or yellow construction paper; one small 5-oz. styrofoam cup; paint, scissors, stapler, white glue.

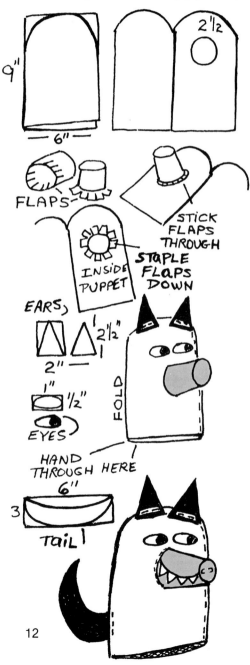

9″

6″

2½

FLAPS

STICK FLAPS THROUGH

STAPLE FLAPS DOWN

INSIDE PUPPET

EARS

2½″

2″

1″

½″

EYES

FOLD

HAND THROUGH HERE

6″

3

Tail

Before you make your puppet, put Wolf's nose in place. Fold the 9″ × 12″ felt in half to make 6″ × 9″ puppet body. Round off corners but do not staple closed. Paint the styrofoam cup gray and let it dry. You may need more than one coat of paint. When it's dry, measure 2½″ down from top middle of one half of body piece, mark a dot, and trace the bottom of the cup on it. Cut out the circle. Make ½″ flaps with scissors all around rim of cup. Stick flaps through hole. Staple all flaps to puppet body. Now staple top and side of puppet closed.

Draw triangle ears on the 2″ × 2½″ gray or black pieces and cut out. Staple to top of puppet for ears. Draw wide oval eyes on the 1″ × ½″ white or yellow pieces and cut out. Paint pupils black. Glue to Wolf.

On each side of cup, paint a curved line for Wolf's grin with a few white pointed teeth under it. Draw a skinny crescent moon shape for a tail on the 6″ × 3″ felt. Cut out and staple to back of puppet (not through to front) by a tiny flap.

ALEX THE ALLIGATOR

You need: a 9″ × 12″ piece of green craft felt; two 1″ × 2″, two 4″ × 4½″, and one 2″ × 6″ strip of heavyweight yellow construction paper; paints, scissors, stapler, white glue.

Fold felt in half to form a 6″ × 9″ puppet, but do not round off corners as on other puppets. Before you staple your puppet closed, put its jaw in place. Draw a ½″ border around both 4″ × 4½″ pieces with a pencil. From each corner on both pieces, cut a diagonal slit to inner corners of the border line. Fold up your border edges to form a box with jagged corners. Look at picture. Cut pointed teeth all along sides and front of boxes. Paint teeth white. Let dry. Staple or tape the two back edges together by placing one edge of the box on top of the other along the straight back edge to form jaw shape. Open stapler and tack flat back of jaw to front and center of puppet, about 2″ down from top. Be sure to bend over staple points on back of felt so they won't scratch your hand. You can use white glue if it is easier for you. Staple the side of puppet closed. Now cut two mounds at top and staple closed all along the top.

Draw oval eyes on the 1″ × 2″ pieces and cut out. Paint pupils black. Glue one eye below each mound. Paint nostrils on box (above teeth) as in picture.

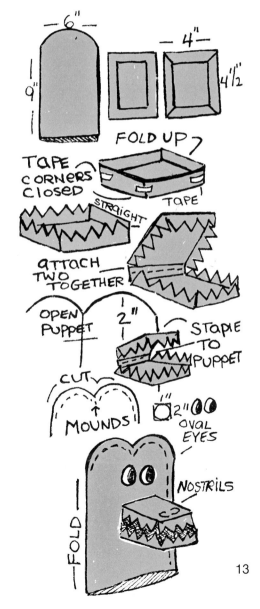

13

Draw about 5 scallops on one edge of the 2″ × 6″ yellow strip and cut along the line. Form a ¼″ border by bending the opposite edge. Glue tail to Alligator as in picture. Paint some spots on it and on the front of the Alligator if you like.

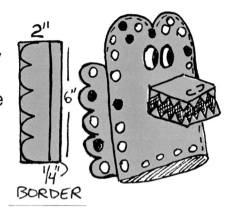

2″

6″

¼″
BORDER

THE GOOD WITCH

You need: a 9″ × 12″ piece of white or beige craft felt; one 3½″ × 1½″ piece of green construction paper; two 6″ × 5½″ pieces, one 7″ × 5½″ piece, two 2″ × 3½″ pieces, and two 2″ × 2¾″ pieces of black construction paper; sixteen ½″ × 3½″ strips of yellow or orange crepe paper; paints, stapler, scissors, white glue.

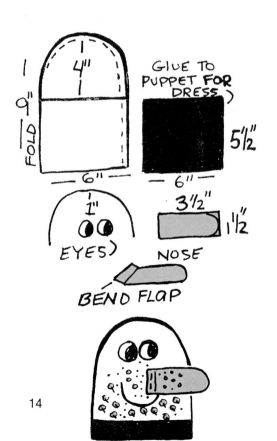

4″

FOLD 9″

6″

GLUE TO PUPPET FOR DRESS

5½

6″

3½″ 1½

1″

EYES

NOSE

BEND FLAP

Make the puppet's body in the same way as the other puppets. Fold the 9″ × 12″ felt in half and round off the top corners. Measure 4″ down from the top and draw a straight line across. Glue one 6″ × 5½″ black piece to the front and one to the back of the puppet for the witch's dress. About 1″ down from the top of the puppet's head, paint nickel-size eyes with pupils.

With scissors, round off a corner of one edge of the 3½″ × 1½″ green piece. Bend a small flap at straight end and glue or staple to puppet below eyes for nose. Paint a broad grin under the nose, with some boils and some mole hairs on chin if you like.

Paint buttons down the dress. Staple tops of crepe paper strips to sides and back of puppet's head for hair. Staple a 2″ × 3½″ black piece diagonally to each side of puppet for sleeves.

For hat: Make a dot at the top middle of the 7″ × 5½″ black piece. Measure 3″ down each side and mark dots. Then measure 2½″ down each side and mark two more dots. Connect all the dots in a hat shape as in picture, with a curved line from side dots that touches the bottom. Cut out. Staple hat to top of witch's head.

KING TREE TROLL AND THE TERRIBLE TREE TROLLS

You make all the Tree Trolls the same, except the king who wears a crown. For the Trolls, you use a narrower width of craft felt than for the other puppets.

For each Troll, *you need:* a 9″ × 10″ piece of brown craft felt; black paint, scissors, stapler. For the King, *you also need:* one 5″ × 1½″ piece of yellow construction paper. Make as many Trolls as you like.

Fold the piece of felt and close top and side with stapler. About 2″ down from top, cut two holes for your fingers to go through as gnarled branches. Paint tree gnarls all over front and back of puppet.

For the King's crown: Draw a line across the middle of the 5″ × 1½″ yellow piece. From line, draw triangle

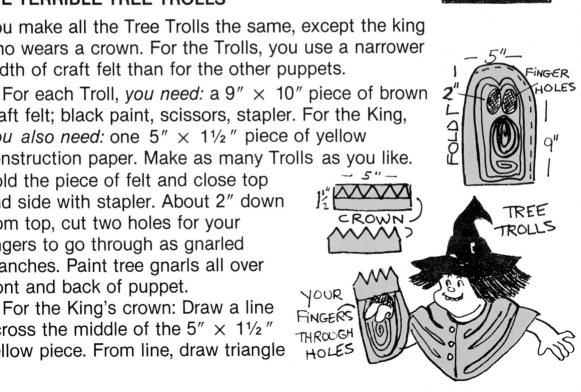

points that touch the edge. Cut out. Staple to top of puppet for King Tree Troll's crown.

After your puppets are made, you are ready to rehearse your puppet play. A table can be used for your stage, but it must be big enough for all the puppeteers to hide under. A picnic table is good. Cover it with a large sheet or tablecloth.

STORE PUPPETS iN LaTER

OPEN END ON TOP

To make a barn for your stage, paint a medium-sized grocery carton red. Then paint a large brown barn door and window on the front of it. Stand it on your table. Store your puppets in it when you are not using them.

This is the name of the play:

The Barnyard Puppets and the Spell of the Terrible Tree Trolls

This is what the story is about (the basic plot). You can make up your own dialogue (what the puppets say) as you go along.

The Good Witch and all of her barnyard animals live peacefully together. However, King Tree Troll is very jealous because they are so happy. He wants everyone to be as miserable as he and his Tree Trolls are. So when the Good Witch goes out of town, he sends one of his terrible Tree Trolls over to spread sleeping dust on the barnyard animals, so they will fall asleep for 100 years and there will be no more laughter and happiness in the barnyard.

Fortunately, Wilson the Wise Owl is up in a tree (leave him off the stage during this time) when the Tree Troll is spreading the sleeping dust and he sees the animals fall asleep. When the Good Witch returns, he tells her what has happened. She goes to King Tree Troll and threatens to turn him and his whole kingdom of terrible Tree Trolls into tiny chipmunks if he doesn't break the spell. He does, and the barnyard animals wake up. Everyone rejoices, Wilson the Wise Owl is rewarded, and King Tree Troll and his Terrible Tree Trolls remain as miserable as ever!

After putting on this play, make up some new ones for your puppets.

The Little Witch and her friends send out their Happy Splashy Duck Invitations (p. 42) about a week before the play. You can also hang an invitation on a church or community bulletin board. Charge 10¢ or 15¢ admission. If you like, make a batch of Honeybee Cookies (p. 41) and Berry Perfect Summer Punch (p. 33) to serve your guests. When they are seated, have one of the puppets appear above the stage to announce the play. Say: "*The Barnyard Summer Puppet Theater presents The Barnyard Puppets and the Spell of the Terrible Tree Trolls.*" Don't forget to rehearse your play.

SUMMERTIME COUNTRY FAIR

The night before the Country Fair, the Little Witch and the Goblin put the finishing touches on their Pet Pigs. They bake Prize Winning Blueberry Muffins and Natural Nut Roll-ups in the Goblin's kitchen to sell and exhibit at the Country Fair. Some other things to sell at the fair are: Caterpillar Bookmarks (p. 27), Little Tugboat Sandwich Carriers (p. 26), Seashell Craft Creatures (p. 45), Night Owl Snack Box (p. 30) filled with a few Honeybee Cookies (p. 41), and Mr. C. Gull (p. 43).

All you need for a Country Fair is some space and a few tables to exhibit your goods. The money you earn can go to your favorite charity or wildlife fund, or save it in your Pet Pig bank toward back-to-school money.

Send out a few Friendly Frog Invitations to let your friends know about the fair. Post one on a community bulletin board. You can also sell Friendly Frogs at the fair as bathroom or kitchen decorations (do not write a message on them). They can be a "Do Not Disturb" sign for your door. Tie a 12″ string through a hole at top to hang.

FRIENDLY FROG INVITATIONS

For each frog, *you need:* one 5″ × 9½″ piece and one 7″ × 5¼″ piece of heavyweight construction paper; four 3¼″ × 2½″ pieces and two 1½″ × 1½″ pieces of yellow construction paper; paint, scissors, stapler.

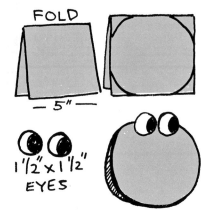

FOLD

— 5″ —

1½″ × 1½″
EYES

Fold length of 5″ × 9½″ green piece in half with fold at top. Round off top and bottom corners with scissors. Draw circles on the 1½″ × 1½″ yellow pieces and cut out. Paint pupils. Staple to fold at top for eyes.

Paint some nostrils about 1½" below eyes. Draw a wide oval on the 7" × 5¼" piece. Cut out. Open the frog's head and staple about 2" of bottom of inner piece to frog's 7" × 5¼" body. Just staple inner piece so card opens. See picture.

Look at picture. Draw a frog leg on each 3½" × 2½" yellow piece to look like a puzzle piece. Cut out. Staple two legs to front, under frog's jaw, and two to bottom. Paint spots on frog. Bend top flap in half at nostrils, then open all the way to write message: Dear _____. Come to a Summer Country Fair, Saturday, _____. Time: _____. At: Goblin's House. Lots to buy and eat!

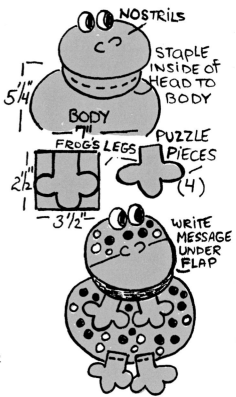

ALL PURPOSE PET PIGS

The Little Witch and Goblin make pet pigs to sell at the fair. You can name your pig Sarah or Sally or Ethel or Harry. Some real pigs weigh as much as 900 pounds. The Pet Pigs that the Little Witch and Goblin make can be piggy banks to hold money, cookie jars (wrap cookies first), lunch boxes (but, not on rainy days), or a picnic basket, if you staple a 20″ string or ribbon to the sides for a handle.

For each pig, *you need:* one 15″ × 8½″ piece and one 5″ × 5″ piece of white posterboard; two 2″ × 3½″ pieces and four 1½″ × 2″ pieces of pink construction paper; a 5-oz. styrofoam cup; paints, stapler, tape; a pipe cleaner.

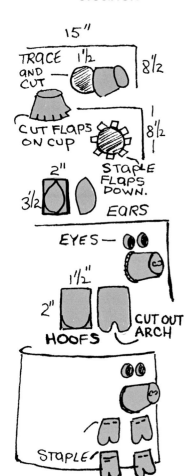

Trace rim of cup 1½″ down from top of 15″ × 8½″ piece of white posterboard and cut out circle. Tape and staple cup well to inside to form pig's nose.

Draw the tear shape on each 2″ × 3½″ piece as in picture, for ears. Cut out. Staple to sides of 15″ × 8½″ cylinder piece. Paint dime-size eyes above nose. Paint your cup pink or beige, then paint two nostrils in front. Round off bottom corners on each 1½″ × 2″ piece. Then cut out a little arch in front for Pig's hoofs. Tape and staple two legs at bottom front and two about 3″ up from bottom as in picture. Twist your pipe cleaner in a ringlet shape and staple to back, 2″ up from bottom.

Roll the 15 × 8½″ piece in a cylinder. Staple and tape closed very well. To close pig, carefully trace bottom rim of cylinder on 5″ × 5″ posterboard. Then draw a circle about ⅛″ outside it. When cut, circle should be a bit larger than rim, just enough to squeeze through top and down toward bottom of pig to close bottom. It does not have to fit all the way to bottom, but it must fit tightly in pig, so it won't fall through and it will hold your items. If you want to name your pig, paint name on a piece of colored construction paper cut in a circle, then staple circle to bottom or top of pig cylinder. Be sure to make a sign on posterboard to put on your table that says, "All Purpose Pet Pigs: Banks, Cookie Jars, Picnic Baskets, Lunch Boxes. 35¢ to 50¢."

GOBLIN'S NATURAL FOOD STAND

The Goblin sets up a natural food stand at the fair. He sells Prize Winning Blueberry Breakfast Muffins (10¢ each) and Natural Nut Roll-ups (5¢ each) for people with a sweet tooth (but they are made out of natural ingredients).

Natural Nut Roll-ups

1 cup peanut butter	¼ cup raisins
¼ cup chopped dates	½ cup nonfat dry milk powder
¼ cup sesame seeds	¼ cup honey

Mix all together, roll in 1″ balls, refrigerate. Do not remove from refrigerator until you are ready to leave for the fair. Makes about 10 small balls.

21

Prize Winning Blueberry Muffins

At the fair, some people like to exhibit their homemade prize winning recipes. The Little Witch and Goblin's Blueberry Muffins are especially good because blueberries are plentiful in their area.

2 tbsps. melted butter   3 tsps. baking powder
2 tbsps. brown sugar   ¾ cup milk
2 cups wholewheat flour   1 cup dry blueberries

Mix butter and sugar together. Add to dry ingredients and mix well. Pour in milk, add blueberries. Mix quickly. If too dry, add ¼ cup more milk. Fill buttered muffin tins about ⅔ from top. Bake at 400° about 25 minutes. Makes twelve muffins.

FAVORITE SUMMERTIME GATHERINGS

Picnics
Parties
Pastimes

LAZY SUMMER DAY CLOUD PICNIC

The Little Witch and her friends like to have a Lazy Summer Day Cloud Picnic, to relax, have a picnic lunch, and read their favorite summer books. Everyone should wear an Upside-Down Cloud Hat and bring lunch in a Little Tugboat Sandwich Carrier. A friend can help you get everything ready for the picnic. Invite 3 or 4 friends and make each guest a hat, a Tugboat Sandwich Carrier, and a Caterpillar Bookmark. Be sure to tell your friends to bring their favorite books. Send out your invitations a few days earlier, and make your recipes the day of the party.

SUMMER CLOUD INVITATIONS

Fold the width of a 10″ × 3″ piece of white construction paper in half. Draw the cloud shape on it, as in picture. Cut out. Do not cut fold. Open and write message: Dear _____, You are invited to a Lazy Summer Day Cloud Picnic, Friday, July _____, at _____ AM. Place _____. Bring your favorite book. Do not forget!

UPSIDE-DOWN CLOUD HAT

Make a hat for each guest.

For each hat *you need:* an 18″ × 8″ piece of blue heavyweight construction paper; five 6″ × 3″ and one 10″ × 10″ pieces of white heavyweight construction paper; five 8″ pieces of heavy white thread; two 5″ strings; scissors, tape.

Roll the 18″ × 8″ blue piece in a cylinder. Overlap 2″. Staple and tape seam closed. Draw a full circle on the 10″ × 10″ white piece. Cut out. Trace rim of cylinder in center. Cut out on lines. Cut ½″ flaps all around cylinder bottom. Slip flaps through hole on the 10″ × 10″ piece. Staple or tape flaps securely to rim. See picture. Stand hat upside down.

Draw cloud shape on each 6″ × 3″ white piece and cut out. Mark five dots lightly on underside of hat brim ½″ from edge and about 6″ apart (to hang clouds). Make a tiny hole with a pencil point on each cloud. Pass the end of a thread through each hole and knot it. Tape the other end of each thread to a dot you marked under hat rim. Staple a 5″ string to each side of hat cylinder and tie under chin.

25

LITTLE TUGBOAT SANDWICH CARRIER

Each guest gets a tugboat to carry a sandwich and cookies in.

For each tugboat *you need:* two 9″ × 5½″ pieces of red heavyweight construction paper; a 4″ × 4″ piece of blue construction paper; a 1½″ × 2½″ piece of yellow or white construction paper; a 2″ × 2½″ piece of black heavyweight construction paper; stapler, scissors, tape, yellow paint, white glue.

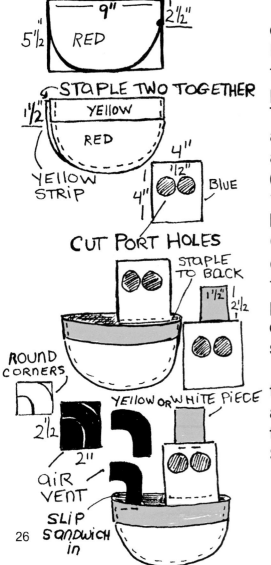

Measure 2½″ down from right side of one 9″ × 5½″ red piece. Mark dot. Make a curve from left corner that touches bottom and up to dot as in picture. Cut along curve to form boat. Trace boat shape on other red piece and cut out. Staple the two together along side and bottom, not top (sandwich will slip in later). Paint a 1½″ yellow strip all along top of red boat on front and back as in picture. Cut two quarter-size circles about ½″ down from top of 4″ × 4″ blue piece for portholes. Staple bottom of blue piece to top of back piece of boat only (not through to front) so sandwich slips in.

Staple the 1½ × 2½″ white piece to top of cabin. Look at the picture and draw the Tugboat's air vent on the 2″ × 2½″ black piece. Cut out. Staple to front piece of boat only.

26

Give each friend a wrapped sandwich and a few Honeybee cookies (p. 41) to carry in the boat. Later it can hold school papers, letters, kitchen recipes, pencils and pens, photos, etc.

TOMATO CHEESE SANDWICHES

Make one for each friend. Take two slices of firm white or wholewheat bread. Cover one slice with a layer of mayonnaise. Then add a slice of cheese (American, Swiss, or your favorite). Top with a slice of tomato and the other slice of bread. Cut in half. Wrap in foil.

Bring two cups of Little Witch's Garden Potato Salad (p. 37) in a jar or covered container, along with little cans of your favorite fruit juice. Put everything in a Cloud Box (a shoe box painted blue with white clouds painted on it). Take turns with your friends carrying it to the picnic spot. Don't forget paper plates, forks, napkins. Throw all your used plates in a trash can or bring them home in the Cloud Box. Pick a nice picnic spot, like a park or schoolyard with a shady tree. You may want to bring a picnic blanket or sheet. Distribute the lunch, in portions, for each friend.

Give each friend a Caterpillar Bookmark. After lunch, take turns reading your favorite pages to each other.

CASEY THE CATERPILLAR BOOKMARK

Use Casey to keep your place in your book. On another day the Little Tugboat can carry a paperback.

To make Casey, *you need:* six 2″ × 2″ squares of posterboard; yellow, orange, and black paint; four paper fasteners; two 3½″ pieces of pipe cleaner; scissors, stapler.

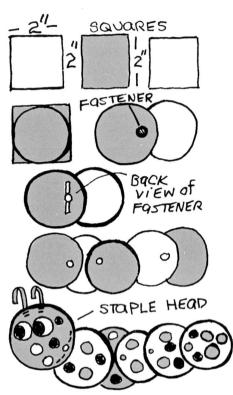

Paint two squares orange, two yellow, and two black. Let dry. Draw a circle that touches the edges on each square. Cut out. Attach five circles (leave sixth aside) together at edges with paper fasteners. See picture. Alternate your colors: orange, then yellow, then black, and so on. Attach the sixth circle, which is the head, to top of fifth circle with a staple (not a fastener). Paint dime-size eyes on it. Staple pieces of pipe cleaner to head above eyes for feelers. Paint some spots of different colors on Casey, if you like.

NIGHT OWL PARTY AND FIREFLY BALL

On summer nights the Little Witch and her friends gather together for the Night Owl Party and Firefly Ball. It is nice to have about four or five people at the party. Everyone should come as a firefly. You do not have to have the party at night. You can have it during the day in a dark, cool basement. But it is more fun outdoors when it starts to get dark. The Little Witch and her friends eat Owl and Firefly Snacks and play the Owl Whoo? game. You can make and read Tombstone Thrillers (p. 48) also.

Send out your Night Owl Invitations in advance of the party. Set a date to meet at your house a day or two before the party to make the costumes. Tell each friend to bring a medium-size grocery bag and some yellow paint. You can supply everything else, with the help of another friend.

NIGHT OWL INVITATIONS

For each, *you need:* one 8″ × 7″ piece and two 2″ × 1½″ pieces of brown construction paper; a 2″ × 3″ piece of orange construction paper; a 3″ × 3″ piece of light colored construction paper; paint, scissors, stapler.

Round off top corners of 8″ × 7″ brown piece with scissors. Cut jagged edges down each side about ½″ deep for owl's feathers. Draw a triangle on each 2″ × 1½″ brown piece. Cut out. Staple to top of head for ears. Paint large eyes the size of a half dollar about 1″ down from ears.

Draw triangle on 2″ × 3″ orange piece as in picture. Cut out. Staple below owl's eyes, along 2″ edge.

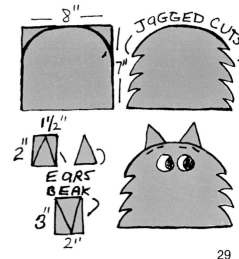

STAPLE TOP ONLY

SLIP MESSAGE UNDER BEAK

Write your message on the 3″ × 3″ paper and slip it under the beak. Deliver the invitations to your friends' houses.

Dear Kyle, You are invited to a NIGHT OWL PARTY and FIREFLY BALL, Saturday, July _____, Time _____, at: Little Witch's House. Come over, Friday, at 2:00 to make your Firefly costume. Bring a medium-size grocery bag and a jar of yellow poster paint.

If a friend cannot come over to make the costume, he or she can copy directions down at an earlier date and make it at home.

The Little Witch puts several snacks around in Night Owl Boxes for the Fireflies to munch on. The boxes are similar to the Night Owl Invitations.

NIGHT OWL SNACK BOX

For each box, *you need:* a 12″ × 12″ piece of posterboard, painted green or orange; a 5″ × 5″ piece of brown heavyweight construction paper; two 1″ × 1″ pieces and one 6″ × 6″ piece of orange construction paper; one 1″ × 1½″ piece and two 3″ × 2″ pieces of yellow construction paper; white glue, stapler, scissors, paint, tape.

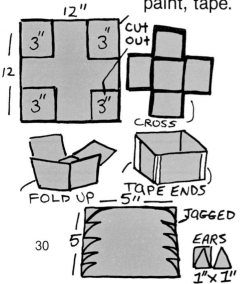

Measure a 3″ square out of each corner of the 12″ × 12″ posterboard piece. Cut out the four squares to make a cross shape. Fold squares up to form a box. Tape corners of box closed very well. Cut jagged edges on sides of 5″ × 5″ brown piece as you did for the invitations. Round off top corners. Draw triangle ears on the 1″ × 1″ orange pieces. Staple to top of the 5″ × 5″ piece.

About ¾″ down from top, paint nickel-size owl eyes in white or yellow with dark pupils. Draw triangle beak on the 1″ × 1½″ yellow piece. Cut out. Staple below eyes.

To make wings: Draw a circle on the 6″ × 6″ orange piece. Cut it in half. Staple a wing at each side and back of owl as in picture. Now glue bottom half of owl to box front. Head will stick up above box, as in picture, and wings will extend out to sides.

To make feet: Draw the owl's claw shape on the 3″ × 2″ yellow pieces, as in the picture. Be sure to leave a flat space at top for flap. Cut out. Tape flat part under box, so three claw points extend out in front. Paint some "V" and "U" feather markings on wings and body.

Put your salads and snacks in bowls before you place them in the Night Owl Snack Box. Line bottom of Owl Snack Box with aluminum foil first. Put your cookies in bowls also. Later your Owl Box can hold a potted plant or Halloween snacks at a Halloween party.

FIREFLY COSTUME

When your friends come over to make their costumes be sure everyone has brought a brown grocery bag. You can share paint. Gather together the supplies you will need.

For each costume, *you need:* two 12″ × 18″ pieces and one 24″ × 2½″ strip (staple two 12″ × 2½″ strips together to get a 24″ strip) of brown heavyweight construction paper; one 24″ × 1″ strip of yellow construction paper (again, staple two 12″ strips together); three large safety pins, two pipe cleaners; staplers, scissors, yellow paint.

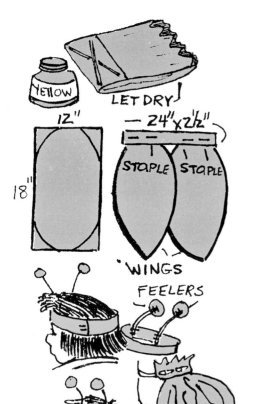

YELLOW
LET DRY
12″
18″
— 24″x2½″ —
STAPLE   STAPLE
WINGS
FEELERS
PIN
BAG
TO
REAR

First lay your paper bag out flat with bottom tucked under. If the bag has printing on it, turn it inside out. Paint both sides and bottom yellow, and let dry.

Round off each corner of the 12″ and 18″ brown pieces, as in picture. Cut out on lines for wings. Staple each wing to a 24″ × 2½″ brown strip.

To make headband: Fit the 1″ × 24″ strip around your head until it sits above your eyebrows. Overlap and staple closed. Staple a quarter-size piece of yellow construction paper to each pipe cleaner tip, then staple other end behind front of strip for firefly feelers, as in picture.

To complete your costume, wear old pants or shorts and leotards and a T-shirt or old shirt. Put sneakers or slippers on your feet. Wear the headband around your head. Have a friend pin the strip that holds the wings across the back of your shirt. Fluff out the bag as if you were going to pop it, then fold and staple opening closed. Pin three spots to rear. Wear gloves and sunglasses to complete your costume if you like.

FIREFLY SNACKS

Serve these munchies at the party.

Owl's Olive Walnut Salad

1 cup celery chopped in small pieces
¼ cup olives (without pits) chopped in thin slices
¼ cup walnuts chopped fine
½ cup whipped cream cheese
Mix all together if you want a creamier dip-like spread. Put in a bowl, then in your Night Owl Snack Box. Spread on graham crackers or your favorite cracker.

Firefly's Apple Nut Crunch Cookies

3 cups rolled oats	1 cup wholewheat flour
1 cup apple juice	1 cup raisins
¼ tsp. cinnamon	½ cup chopped nuts
1 cup warm water	

Mix oats, flour, and juice in a large bowl until lumps are gone. Stir in cinnamon and raisins. Add warm water. Let stand 20 minutes. Mix again well. Drop by spoonfuls, then flatten on lightly greased cookie sheet. Bake at 350° for 35 minutes.

Berry Perfect Summer Punch

In a large pitcher mix 2 cups lemonade, 2 cups ginger ale, and 1 cup cranberry juice. Shake well and serve over ice. Makes about five ½-cup servings. Good for thirsty fireflies.

OWL WHOO? COUNTING GAME

The Owl Whoo? counting game is a tongue-twister but it is fun to play at the party.

It is a number game. For each "two," you must substitute "whoo" instead. Gather the players together. Someone starts off the counting with "one," the next player says "whoo" instead of "two." You keep counting. The next time "two" comes up, it is in the number 12, so you say "ten-whoo" for twelve. Keep counting. Next comes 20, which must be "whooty." Then 22 is "whooty whoo," 27 is "whooty seven," and so on. The idea is to say "whoo" every time "two" comes in a number. When a player misses, he or she drops from the game. Keep playing until one player is left, the winner. The number 222, if you get that far, is "whooty whoo whoo!"

FOURTH OF JULY SPARKLE PARTY

(An Eat Outdoor Day)

The Little Witch and her friend Goblin, the natural chef, plan a Fourth of July Sparkle Party to celebrate Independence Day (July 4, 1776) when the Declaration of Independence was signed and the American colonies announced their right to be free from England.

They get together with friends and relatives to eat outdoors and share some of their favorite summer foods. Send your Star Invitations out a few days before the party. The Goblin helps the Little Witch make the recipes.

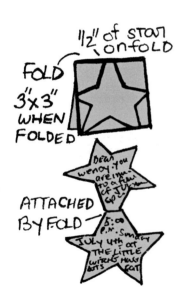

½" of STAR on FOLD

FOLD
3"x3"
WHEN
FOLDED

ATTACHED BY FOLD

STAR INVITATIONS

Fold the length of a 6″ × 6″ piece of yellow construction paper in half. Draw the five-pointed star on it by copying the picture. It does not have to be perfect. All stars are different. You must be sure, however, that at least ½″ of top point of star is on the fold so it will open as a card after it is cut. Cut out on your lines through both pieces (not on fold). Open card and write message. Dear <u>Wendy,</u> You are invited to a Fourth of July Sparkle Party, <u>5:00 P.M.,</u> <u>Sunday,</u> July 4th at: <u>Little Witch's.</u> Lots to eat!

Make a Star Sparkler to give each guest. It is fun to twirl to celebrate the holiday. No real firecrackers are allowed at the party!

STAR SPARKLER

For each one, *you need:* a 12″ × ¾″ strip of cardboard, painted gold or yellow on both sides; a 5″ × 5″ piece of cardboard painted the same color; assorted paints: pink, purple, orange; six 7″ × ¼″ strips of crepe color (any color); stapler, scissors, paper fastener.

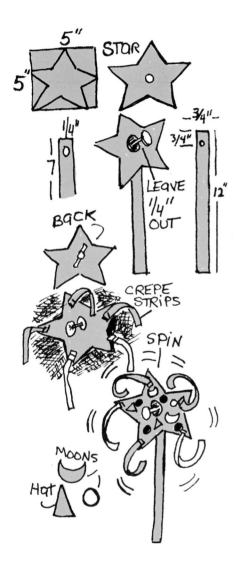

Draw star shape (as on the invitation) on the 5″ × 5″ cardboard. In center of star punch a tiny hole with scissors (have an adult do it). Punch another hole ¾″ from one end of cardboard strip. Put paper fastener through both holes to attach star to strip. When you put fastener through star and strip, do not press it all the way down. Leave about ¼″ of its head sticking out in front, so star twirls on it. See picture.

Bend fastener's legs down in back. Staple a crepe paper strip to each star point and paint witches' full and crescent moons and goblins' hats all over front and back of star with the assorted colors of paint. If your star doesn't spin, stick your paper fastener out more in front.

The Little Witch and Goblin prepare their traditional Fourth of July recipes earlier in the day at Goblin's house. If you would like to have some hot dogs at the party (have an adult cook them), Crunchy Corn Relish is a good topping, and Berry Perfect Summer Punch (p. 33) is nice to drink.

CRUNCHY CORN RELISH

2 cups whole kernel corn (fresh or drained from can)
½ cup sweet red pepper chopped in tiny pieces
2 tbsps. pickle relish   1 tsp. apple cider vinegar
1 tsp. honey

Mix all well in a bowl. Store in a covered container or jar. Spoon over hot dogs.

GOBLIN'S CARROT SALAD SLAW

(Serves 4 or 5)

2 cups shredded carrot   ½ cup mayonnaise
¼ cup raisins   ½ cup crushed pineapple
1 tsp. honey

Mix all together very well in a medium-size bowl. Add more mayonnaise if needed for moisture.

LITTLE WITCH'S GARDEN POTATO SALAD

(Have an adult do the boiling. Serves 4 or 5.)

3 medium boiled potatoes   1 hard boiled egg
¼ cup radishes sliced very thin   1 cup chopped green pepper
1 tbsp. honey   ½ cup mayonnaise
1 tsp. cider vinegar

Chop potatoes in small cubes. Chop egg in small bits. In large bowl, combine vegetables and all other ingredients. Mix well.

Later in the evening when everyone is watching the Fourth of July fireworks display, Grandmother Witch brings out dishes of her Lemon Summer Night Sherbet and tells everyone a very spooky story.

GRANDMA WITCH'S LEMON SUMMER NIGHT SHERBET

This is a milk sherbet (very creamy) that serves 6 people.
4 cups milk
1½ cups sugar
juice of 3 lemons
Mix juice and sugar, stirring constantly while adding milk slowly. If added too quickly, mixture will look curdled, so go very slow. Freeze and serve.

SPECIAL SUMMER DAYS

SUMMER COLDS

Sometimes you are sick in bed with a summer cold. They are no fun. But when you or a friend get one, here are some of the Little Witch's homemade remedies to cheer things up.

HONEYBEE GET WELL CARD

A Honeybee Get Well Card can make anyone happy, at least temporarily. Send a little bag of Honeybee cookies along with it (p. 41).

For the card, *you need:* a 5″ × 14″ piece of yellow heavyweight construction paper; one 4″ × 4″ piece and two 1″ × 1″ pieces of black construction paper; black paint, stapler, white glue, scissors.

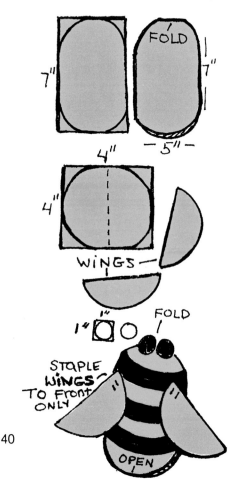

Draw line across the middle of 5″ × 14″ piece to make a 5″ × 7″ piece with fold at top to form card. Round off all four edges with scissors to form a bee shape. Do not cut across your fold. Draw a circle on the 4″ × 4″ black piece. Cut out, then cut in half. With curves facing inward, staple tip of each half to side of bee for wings. Staple to front piece of card only. Paint a few curved stripes in black on body of bee as in picture. Draw a circle on each 1″ × 1″ piece. Cut out. Staple to top fold of bee. Open card. Write message.

Dear Paul. Sorry to hear you aren't feeling well. Hope you will be buzzing around like a bee soon. Here are some Honeybee Cookies to cheer you up.

Wrap up two or three Honeybee Cookies in plastic wrap like a sack and staple to the inside of your card. This also makes a nice summer birthday card.

HONEYBEE COOKIES
(20 to 30 small cookies)

1¼ cups wholewheat flour 1 tsp. baking soda
½ cup honey 1 tsp. vanilla
1 beaten egg ⅓ cup melted butter or oil
½ cup raisins ½ cup chopped nuts

Mix dry ingredients in a large bowl. Mix butter, honey, vanilla, and egg well in another bowl. Add to dry ingredients. Add raisins and nuts, mix well. Drop by spoonfuls on ungreased cookie sheet. Bake at 375° for 12 minutes. Wrap when cool.

HAPPY SPLASHY DUCK CARD

Summer is a happy season for ducks, especially during summer showers. Here is a Happy Splashy Duck Card to give as a get-well card or for a summer birthday. Birth signs for summer birthdays are:

Cancer, the Crab: June 22 to July 22

Leo, the Lion: July 23 to August 23

For each card, *you need:* one 4½″ × 7″ piece and one 3″ × 1¾″ piece of yellow heavyweight construction paper; two 4½″ × 3″ pieces of white construction paper; a 2″ × 3″ piece of any color construction paper; paint, stapler, scissors.

Round off top corners of the 4½″ × 7″ yellow piece with scissors. Round off corners on one end of the 3″ × 1¾″ yellow piece. Staple that to side of 4½″ × 7″ piece as in picture, for duck's bill, about 1½″ down from top. Paint two round eyes above it, as in picture.

On each 4½″ × 3″ white piece, draw the scalloped diagonal line from left bottom to top right. Cut out on lines. Staple one wing to each side about 2″ in from edges, one to front and one to back, so message can be held between wings. Write your message on the 2″ × 3″ paper and flip between wings. Write either *Get Well* or *Happy Birthday*. This is also the invitation to the Puppet Play. Write the name of the play and date, time, and place where it will be given.

MR. C. GULL TISSUE HOLDER
(For summer colds and other uses)

Mr. C. Gull is a nice gift to give someone who has summer sniffles. It holds tissues. It is also a good project to make in bed if you have a cold.

You need: one 8″ × 10″ piece of white posterboard; one 4″ × 4″ piece; one 4″ × 5½″ piece, and one 4½″ × 6″ piece of white heavyweight construction paper; one 6½″ × 3½″ piece and one 4″ × 4″ piece of black construction paper; one 4″ × 4″ piece of orange construction paper; two 2½″ × 2″ pieces of yellow construction paper; scissors, tape, stapler, paints.

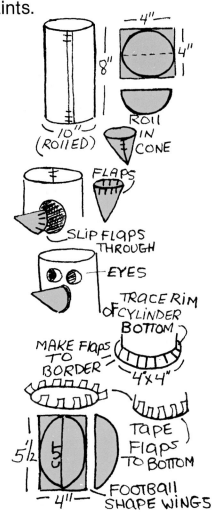

Roll the 8″ × 10″ posterboard in a cylinder. Staple and tape seam firmly closed. Draw a circle on the 4″ × 4″ orange piece. Cut out. Cut circle in half. Roll in small cone. Staple seam closed for beak. Measure 2″ down from cylinder top and trace beak rim in center. Cut out the circle. Cut small ½″ flaps on beak. Slip through hole in cylinder and tape down well to inside. Paint two dime-size eyes above it. To close cylinder bottom: trace it on 4″ × 4″ white paper. Look at picture. All around excess border circle make tiny flaps. Cut and bend flaps. Place circle over bottom of cylinder. Draw the football shape on the 4″ × 5½″ white piece. Cut in half down middle of length for two side wings.

Staple or tape to sides of cylinder as in picture. For tail feathers: Draw a curved line on 4½″ × 6″ white paper

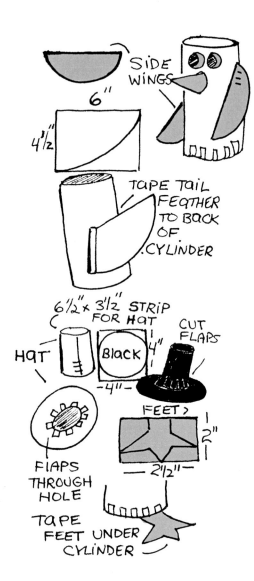

SIDE WINGS

6"

4½"

TAPE TAIL FEATHER TO BACK OF CYLINDER

6½" x 3½" STRIP FOR HAT

HAT

Black

4"

—4"—

CUT FLAPS

FLAPS THROUGH HOLE

FEET

2"

—2½"—

TAPE FEET UNDER CYLINDER

from bottom left corner to top right. Cut on lines. Bend flat end on left side to make ½" strip border. Tape this to back of gull as in picture. Make sure you use enough tape (use clear tape) to attach it well.

To make hat: Roll the 6½" × 3½" black piece in a cylinder. Tape closed. Draw a circle on the 4" × 4" black piece. Cut out. Cut flaps on bottom of cylinder. Slip flaps through circle and tape down. Place hat on gull.

To make feet: Draw the puzzle shape on each 2½" × 2" yellow piece as in picture. Cut out. Tape flat edges underneath cylinder bottom for gull's feet. Fill Mr. C. Gull with tissues. For Christmas, make his hat out of green construction paper. Do not make tail feathers. Paint his wings and his back black and you will have a penguin. He can hold lots of things.

PUT TISSUE IN CYLINDER UNDER HAT

PENGUIN FOR WINTER

(GREEN) HAT

BEACHCOMBING: SEASHELL CREATURES

You can be a summertime artist with shells. When the Little Witch, Goblin, and Owl go to the shore they love to go beachcombing for shells. Dusk or low tide is a good time to collect shells. Do not touch shells with live creatures in them or sea urchins, jellyfish, crabs, etc. They may sting, or you may hurt them.

The Little Witch and Goblin make some very easy shell craft creatures from common shells. You do not need to find the exact shell; just find one that looks like it. Some craft stores sell packages of shells ready to use. Here are some of the shell shapes to look for.

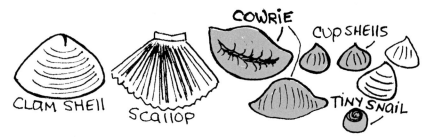

All of these shells come in many sizes and shapes—small, medium, and large (3″ and over). Some cup shells are as small as the ones pictured. Bring a container to store your shells in. Pick ones in good condition.

When you get home, wash your shells with soap and water and let them dry on newspaper. Here are some of the things you need to make shell creatures: pipe cleaners, shells, cotton pieces, tempera paints, model cement or white glue. Glue must be put on thick and must set until thoroughly dry.

FROG ON A LILY PAD

You need: four clam or scallop shells; two 2″ or 3″ wide cup shells and two smaller cup shells, about 1½″ wide; two tiny snail shells or pebbles for the eyes; a 3″ × 2″ piece of yellow or brown craft felt or construction paper; tempera paints, glue, cotton.

First paint all four clam or scallop shells green. Let dry. Attach the two larger shells together (the body) by putting a thick layer of glue on the back flat edges of shells.

Then put a tiny strip of cotton in between to bond the two shells together, let them set until thoroughly dry. Do not touch to move them about. Do the same with the two smaller pieces for the head. Then attach the two tiny snails or pebbles to the top of the head for eyes with a dab of glue. Let set a few minutes. Attach two cup shells underneath large shell body with cotton and glue the same way. These become the feet, as in picture. Glue the head to body with cotton the same way. See picture. Draw and cut out lily pad on 3″ × 2″ felt or paper. Stand frog on it.

When you get better at shellcraft, try an open-mouth effect on your frog by gluing with shells partially open.

SPOTTED TURTLE

You need: a 2″ clam shell and a cowrie shell (not more than 1″); four tiny cup shells; a ¾″ piece of pipe cleaner; glue, cotton, paints.

Paint clam shell yellow, orange, or green. Paint cowrie another color for head. Let dry. Bond the cowrie (head) to the clam shell with the ¾″ pipe cleaner piece. Put glue on shells and on pipe cleaner (see picture). Let glue set. Glue four cup shells under clam shell for feet. Paint eyes and some spots on body of turtle.

LITTLE WITCH'S OWL WALL PLAQUE

You need: a 6½″ × 8″ piece of cardboard, painted purple, blue, or green; two 2″ scallop shells and four ¾″ to 1″ scallop shells; a 1″ cowrie shell; two small cup shells (for eyes); a 3″ × 4″ rectangle of light brown construction paper; 8″ loop of string; orange and yellow paints, glue.

Paint scallop shells orange and paint cowrie and cup shells yellow. In center of 6½″ × 8″ cardboard, glue the 3″ × 4″ rectangle for owl's body. Glue two 1″ scallop shells at top for ears, and two to bottom for feet. Below ears glue two cup shells for eyes; paint pupils. Below them glue a cowrie for beak. At sides, glue 2″ scallop shells for wings. Paint feather markings on owl. Make a tiny hole at top. Tie the 8″ string through it. Hang on nail. You can also make sea monsters and Martians out of shells.

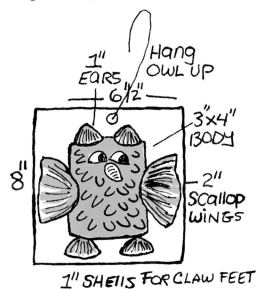

TOMBSTONE THRILLERS
(For summer rainstorms and thunder showers)

During the summer, where Little Witch and Goblin live, there are many rainstorms and thunder showers. On those days they like to get together with friends to tell scary Tombstone Thrillers. They are also fun for the Night Owl Party and at Halloween gatherings.

You need: a 14″ × 12″ piece of light gray construction paper; a 4½″ × 6″ piece of light blue construction paper; three 3″ × 7″ pieces of white typewriter or other thin paper; scissors, stapler, glue.

Fold 14″ × 12″ gray piece in half. Measure 3″ down each side from top, and 1″ in. Mark dot. From dots, make curved lines to top to form tombstone shape. Cut out on lines through both pieces but not on fold. Round off corners on 4½″ × 6″ blue piece. Glue it well to front of tombstone, about 1½″ down from top. Paint on it in large letters: "Here Lies" (your name) or a famous monster in history, and write the dates that the monster lived. You can also stick a photo of yourself or the monster on front. Open tombstone. Staple the three 3″ × 7″ papers together, then to the inside of tombstone. On these papers write your story about the monster named on the front of the tombstone. Change pads for new stories.

Glovach, Linda

The little witch's
summertime book

$10•95

DATE